Mindwaves
the professional writing & communication journal

Editor-in-Chief
Larissa Fleurette Ho

Editors
Andrew Ihamaki
Sandra Nehme
Nathalie Soulliere

Copy Editors
Luke Sawczak
Dylan Smart

Designer
Pu Wen

Editorial Managers
Lily Bowman
Michael Hannon

Faculty Advisor
Robert Price

Special Thanks
Dr. Guy Allen
Dr. Anthony Wensley
Lisa Peden
Diane Pracin
Mubashir Baweja

CONTENT

1   **Foreword**

3   **Preface**

5   **Remembering Tomorrow**
Lyndsay Sinko

17   **Kentucky Hill**
Kevin Ludena

23   **Modern Beatniks**
Jill Kennedy

33   **Belmonts and Carnations**
Samantha Ashenhurst

39   **Rare Cards**
Rob Redford

47	**The Pipe**	
	Matt Spadafora	
53	**Trip to the Taj**	
	Jai Sangha	
61	**Lemon Meringue Pie**	
	Laura Gillis	
67	**Pop Bottle**	
	Dylan Smart	
73	**Lighter**	
	Hiba Traboulsi	
77	**The Blue Cloth**	
	Kristen Loritz	
84	**About the Authors**	

FOREWORD

If you're looking for a good story to read, skip this foreword. All I have to say is thank you.

This is the eighth volume of *Mindwaves*, the creative non-fiction publication of the University of Toronto Mississauga. It exists because of the hard work, bright ideas and vivid storytelling of the university's writers and editors.

The writers in this collection—all students of UTM—produced standout stories. We're grateful to have so many students submit their work for consideration, and we thank the writers in this volume for letting us publish their work.

The editors of this volume deserve special thanks. Led by this year's Editor-in-Chief Larissa Ho, the editorial team generated the call for publications, sorted through a mountainous pile of entries, worked with writers to fine-tune the stories and took care of every aspect of the publication. This is a student venture made possible thanks to the hard work of Larissa, Andrew Ihamaki, Sandra Nehme, Nathalie Soulliere and our design editor Pu Wen. Lily Bowman and Michael Hannon, editors on last year's board, have been on-hand to answer questions and to help put an editorial process in place for next year—thank you.

The people involved in the publication of this volume thank the Institute for Communication, Culture, Information and Technology and the Professional Writing and Communication Program for providing financing and oversight.

Lastly, thank you for supporting new writers by purchasing and reading this collection of stories.

Robert Price
Faculty Advisor, *Mindwaves*
Professional Writing and Communication Program
University of Toronto Mississauga

PREFACE

Writing doesn't just allow me to tell a story. It allows me to feel at peace with the event I'm writing about, as if writing about what happened somehow facilitates the healing of psychological wounds. Storytelling is a therapeutic exercise that builds strength and resilience.

As I read the stories in this volume of *Mindwaves*, I found myself struck by the tenacity of the writers. Kristen Loritz faces her mother's cancer with frustration. Rob Redford writes about a chilling experience in the middle of the night. Lyndsay Sinko realizes she is losing her grandmother to dementia. Their stories paint personal experiences of childhood catastrophe, confusing relationships, family strife, bullying and lived experience with mental illness. Their stories are of pain and suffering.

What's more, in the glimpses we are given into the lives of these writers, the stories have few conventional plotlines—beginnings, middles, and ends. They are simply snapshots in time, pieces of memory. These stories are something to live in, even more than something to tell.

This fact touches on what I think is a vital aspect of the true story: while it is important to share the stories we write, it may be even more important that we write them at all, reliving them and taking part in the cathartic healing process.

But then, through the sharing, we help others live through their own experiences. I know I face stories in my own life that are hard to tell, hard to relive and recount. That's why I continue to write them. I know that the writing heals my own wounds as well as invites the reader to do the same. In this way, the writer's journal becomes the reader's journey.

I am honoured to have the privilege of taking that journey with these writers.

Larissa Fleurette Ho
Editor-in-Chief, *Mindwaves*
March 2014

Remembering Tomorrow
Lyndsay Sinko

"Mom, I don't see them. Are you sure we are at the right terminal?"

I squint at the list of arrivals at the Toronto Pearson International Airport on Wednesday June 5, 2013.

"Yes. Look, it says U.S Airways, Gate 3." Mom checks her gold watch. "They will be here any minute now."

"But what if Nona doesn't remember me?" I say.

It's been over five years since I've seen Nona. I fidget with my phone.

"She's your grandmother. Of course she will remember you." Mom smiles. I smile back and Mom glances at her watch again.

"Mom, look!" I point to the gate and wave. My eyes widen as I see that my aunt is pushing Nona in a wheelchair. I didn't realize that Nona needed a wheelchair.

Nona wriggles and shifts from side to side. I smack my lips and scratch my head, wondering if there is any way I can make her more comfortable.

Nona wears a pink floral Hawaiian T-shirt that contrasts with her Abruzzi skin. Her once-chestnut hair is now pure white but remains short. Her favourite gold hoop earrings dangle from her long earlobes, matching a thin gold cross around her neck. The creases by her dark eyes, sunken against her wrinkled skin, are more defined.

Zia Rosanna wears a simple black T-shirt with fitted jeans, black rectangular framed glasses, white running shoes and a small gold cross necklace. Her hair is gelled in place that keeps her short curls in a tight bob under her ears. I'm still taller than her.

I grin, rush over to them and bend down to embrace Nona first. She still smells like tomatoes.

"Hi, Nona! How are you?" I ask.

"Hi Bella. How are you?" She smiles and kisses my cheek. I catch a flicker of her gold tooth from the corner of her mouth before it disappears. She turns to Mom and beams.

"Laura! E, come stai? How are you?" Nona always says "how are you?" before she discusses the weather. I grin at the familiarity.

Mom bends down to Nona and wraps her arms around her.

"Ma, sto bene! I'm fine. It's good to see you both," Mom says as she grabs Zia Rosanna's suitcase and wheels it to the silver Dodge Journey. Zia Rosanna hugs me and rubs my back. Her hair smells like coconut.

"Hi, love," she says. "You look so much older now. My, have you grown."

"And you're still the exact same, Zia. Still short, but with newer glasses." We giggle and Zia sticks her tongue out at me. I laugh even more and do it back to her. We continue to crack jokes while walking towards the car. Same old Zia. She discusses the flight as I push Nona's wheelchair. Nona hums a merry melody and taps her hand on her knee, the gold earrings swaying from the movement.

Once we reach the car, I help Nona into the back seat and I sit next to her. She smiles at me, humming the same tune as she stares out the window. I glance at her a few times but she never turns away from the window. I sit beside her, only half-listening to Zia's story about the flight. Nona and I don't speak.

Later that night, Mom calls me down to the kitchen. I see opened bags of vegetables covering the marble counter, three pots bubbling on the stovetop, and trays of meat roasting in the oven. A growing pile of dirty dishes fills the sink. Mom mixes something in a bowl with a wooden spoon, Zia slices a circular loaf of bread, and Nona sits in a bar chair at the marble island, staring out the window.

"Lyndsay, can you and Nona start making salad?" Mom asks. "We need help."

"Yeah, that's fine, we will do that now. Hey, Nona," I say and turn to her, "let's make salad."

Nona looks up, shrugs her shoulders and shuffles through the bags of vegetables until she finds the lettuce. She peels leaves of lettuce and rips them into smaller pieces. Her face is blank. I chop cucumbers and tomatoes beside her and toss the vegetables into the red salad bowl as Nona continues to rip the lettuce, almost hypnotically.

"So, Nona, how was your flight?" I ask. She continues to rip and rip and rip the lettuce leaves without answering.

"Nona, how was your flight?" I say louder, and finally, she looks up at me.

"Huh?" She leans her left ear closer to me.

"How was your flight?" I ask even louder.

"Oh, you know. It was good. Nothing special." She starts to hum again, the same cheerful song.

My eyebrows furrow. Mom glances at us, frowns, and then quickly turns back to her sister at the sink. She mutters something I don't understand in Italian to Zia, who looks over at us. Then they are silent for a moment as they chop vegetables. I quickly look down and sulk. After a few silent moments, they go back to chatting loudly about Florida and our relatives. I look up and force a smile at Nona, but she doesn't see me. A few minutes later, Zia calls for me to carry the chicken parmesan out of the oven and place it on the kitchen table.

I parade back and forth from the kitchen to the dining table, balancing bowls of penne pasta in homemade tomato sauce, meatballs, sausages, bruschetta, parmesan cheese and me and Nona's giant salad. What a typical Italian dinner.

At dinner, I sit next to Nona. She grabs my plate and piles it with pasta and salad. More pasta than salad, just as I like it.

"Mangia. Eat." She hands me the plate and sits down. "E bon?" She looks at me expectantly.

"E bon. It's good," I respond, recalling the only slang Italian I know. She strokes my hair with her knobby hands and nibbles the little salad on her plate.

Mom walks over to Nona with a handful of pills, red and blue, green and white, large and small, with a tall glass of water in the other hand.

"Time for your pills, Ma."

Nona takes one pill at a time and gulps down a long sip of water after each one. Mom stands there and waits until all of the coloured pills disappear from her hand.

"Mom, how come Nona doesn't eat much?" I ask, looking from my mountainous plate of penne to Nona's small plate of salad. "She always eats pasta."

"Her pills don't let her eat much," Mom explains and sits across from us. "It's one of the side effects."

Nona hunches over her plate and slowly chews her salad. I rub Nona's back. She continues to blankly stare at the wall above Mom's head. Mom, Zia Rosanna and I discuss school, jobs, family gossip, American politics and the weather for an hour.

Nona remains silent.

※

The next morning, I hear a knock on my bedroom door. The doorknob turns. Bells jingle and claws scrape against hardwood. The sound gets louder until something jumps on me. I jolt from my sleep—what time is it?—and stare at my dog's face. Roxy's tongue flops to the side and she pants. Her stumpy tail whips back and forth, jingling the bell on her collar.

"Lyndsay," Mom says, peeking into my room. "Zia and I need to go shopping for a few hours. Since Jordan and Dad are not here, you have to take care of Nona. We will be back soon."

She slithers away, leaving the door open, as usual.

I sigh and roll out of bed, yawning. I change into an Ed Sheeran T-shirt and sweatpants crumpled in a pile at the end of my bed. I then tie my hair up into a messy bun. Roxy jumps off the queen and scrambles down the stairs to the kitchen where the smell of bacon grows stronger. I follow her.

"Good morning, Nona. How are you?" I wrap both of my arms around her and in return I feel her frail arm around my shoulders briefly.

"Huh? Oh, fine, fine." She turns to the oven and shuts

the burner off. She places the bacon onto a paper towel on the lined beige plate and hums the same upbeat melody she was humming yesterday.

I slump into a bar chair with Nona beside me. I fill a bowl of Oatmeal Crisp cereal with almond milk and Nona nibbles on some toast. Neither of us touches the bacon.

Nona abandons the half piece of toast to finish her orange juice. She stares out the window.

"Nona," I say, "let's go for a walk."

I grab her arm and direct her to the front door. She crosses her Velcro straps, buttons a white sweater and holds her hands in front of her as she waits for me.

I slip on my sandals and glance back at Nona as she slides off her shoes, unbuttons her sweater, and paces back into the kitchen.

"No, Nona. Over here." I chase after her and pull her back to the door.

She smiles and hums.

I attach a leash to Roxy's collar and help Nona out the front door.

"Hey Nona, look at that tree? It's—"

"Lynds, when am I going home?" Nona looks at me.

"Tomorrow," I choke and search for something to distract her with. "So anyways—"

Nona cuts me off and starts to talk in Italian. I nod my head, pretending that I understand her, but she has forgotten that I do not. My stomach turns, as if I'm at the top of a rollercoaster.

"Lynds, when am I going home?" Nona asks again in English.

"Tomorrow. Hey Nona, want to make pizzelles when we get home? You always make the best pizzelles."

She scrunches her face and shrugs her shoulders. I look to the ground.

"Okay, Nona, let's go back home." She wanders behind me and I direct her back to the house. My vision blurs and I wipe my cheek.

❦

I watch The Weather Network in the living room while Nona wheezes loudly on the couch next to me. Her mouth gapes open and a low whistle escapes when she exhales. I can see her gold tooth again.

Her mug of tea is still warm.

The front door swings open and Mom and Zia step into the house hauling large Metro bags full of groceries. They walk to the kitchen and unload. I follow them.

"What did you do with Nona today?" Mom asks as she places a carton of orange juice in the fridge.

"Why does Nona keep asking to go home?" I ask, frowning.

"It's out of her comfort zone, Bella," Zia answers. "Just

keep saying 'tomorrow' when she asks. She won't remember anyways." Zia smiles at me and unloads Ciabatta bread, more orange juice, apple juice, vanilla gelato and salami from one bag. I sit on the bar chair and rest my head on my hands.

"I hate to see her give up so easily," Mom says. "That's not my mom. This miserable old lady is a stranger. All she wants to do is complain and go home." Mom exhales and shakes her head.

"Laura, it's not her fault," Zia says. "You knew she would be this way. She's not happy anywhere except at her house."

My eyes water.

Nona walks into the kitchen, stares blankly at us, and frowns.

"Laura, when am I going home?" she asks.

"Tomorrow," Mom says. "Here, Ma, take these." She opens the cabinet and pulls out a few bottles of pills.

Mom divides the pills: one for calcium, one for iron, one for digestion and two for dementia.

Mom grabs Nona a glass of water. Nona swallows the pills and paces back to the living room. Mom, Zia and I continue to put the groceries away.

I hold Nona and Zia's U.S Airways tickets printed with today's date—Thursday June 20, 2013—in small black numbers at the top right corner. How did these past two weeks go by so fast? I sigh and put the tickets in my jean pocket.

"Is she all packed up? We need to leave!" I call upstairs from the front door. I tie my shoes and look up the stairs.

Nona waddles down the steps and grips the handrail for support. I place my palm under Nona's to help her. Then, I dash upstairs and grab her suitcase. Mom helps Zia with hers and they walk downstairs where Dad and my brother Jordan talk with Nona. I load the trunk with their suitcases while they say goodbye.

I turn my back and quickly wipe away a tear. More tears stream down my face so I wait by the car, inhaling and exhaling. Mom, Zia and Nona walk to the Dodge Journey and I help Nona into the backseat. Zia dabs her eye as she puts on her seatbelt. Then Mom backs out and we drive.

"I'm sure going to miss Jordy. He's such a good boy," Zia says to Mom.

"Oh, I know he'll miss you too. We all will. Next time, we will come down there. It's easier for Mom," Mom replies.

Nona hums.

"Hey, Zia, do you know that song Nona keeps humming?" I ask. "I think I've heard it before."

"Ah, yes, bella. That's the song that she and a bunch of the other children from the village used to sing, back when she lived in Italy. It is a kind of children's song. She sang it to you all the time when you were younger."

I grab Nona's hand and hold it in mine.

"Laura, when am I going home?" Nona asks.

"We are going home now, Ma," Mom replies.

I look over at Nona. She's not staring out the window, but looking back at me. She grins, her gold tooth catching the light, and hums that happy tune.

"Tomorrow" is finally here.

Kentucky Hill
Kevin Ludena

"You sure no one will see us up here?" my best friend Ella asks.

"I'm pretty sure," I answer. "Besides, if you saw people walking here in the middle of the night, would you bother to chase after them?"

"Good point," she says.

I pant and feel a sweat bead form at the tip of my nose. I take one last step and reach the peak.

Ella and I stand on top of Kentucky Hill, a manmade dirt hill that soars almost twenty metres above Lakeshore Road at the edge of Clarkson Village.

"Tell me again why they call this Kentucky Hill?" Ella asks.

"Something about a KFC that was shut down back in the nineties… at least, that's what I grew up hearing," I reply. "Technically, it's called Birchwood Park."

"This neighbourhood's weird," Ella says.

I head over to the old picnic table, take a seat, look

at the horizon, and breath in heavy breaths to calm my nerves. I count the cars that pass by.

One.

Two.

Three.

Ella walks over and takes a seat beside me. I met her last year in my guitar class, when I was in grade ten. She transferred to Blessed Trinity Secondary School from Monseigneur High. The first day of class, she asked me for a piece of paper, a pen she could keep for the rest of the year and a cigarette. I had none of those things.

"So… you sure you want to do this?" she asks me, concern written on her face.

"Can I see it first?" I ask.

"Yeah, of course." She reaches into her brown coat pocket and pulls out a perfectly rolled white joint. It looks like the candy sticks I used to get on Halloween, the ones that come in tiny boxes with the picture of Popeye on the front.

"I'm not going to die from it, am I?" I ask.

"Well, I'm still alive aren't I?"

"Yeah… but you're also brain-dead half the time."

She laughs.

I shiver a little and look at the ground.

"You don't have to if you don't want to," she reminds me. She puts the joint back in her pocket. "Like I said, no pressure."

No pressure, I repeat to myself. I consider telling her to forget about it, and that we should just go to McDonalds, but I don't. I think back to the past two years of high school.

In my mind, I wake up in my tiny bedroom, put on my ugly green uniform, and pack my lunch. On my way to school, I pass by people I know of but never speak to, and ignore them when they call out "loser" or "faggot". I walk through the cramped hallways to get to first period and hear my friends talk about upcoming parties but not invite me. I go home, finish my homework, and then spend a few hours on my laptop. I scroll through Facebook and look at pictures of people at parties, people hanging out, people having fun.

I frown, ball my hands into fists, and squeeze hard. I take a deep breath and close my eyes.

"Fuck it," I tell Ella. "Let's do this."

"I was really hoping you would say that," she says and smiles. She reaches into her coat pocket and fumbles with her Zippo. Then she holds the joint with her mouth and I watch the tip sizzle, blacken, and curl under the flame. She takes a deep drag, holds the smoke in her mouth, looks at me, and exhales. She holds it between her thumb and index finger and passes it to me.

I reach for it, hesitate, and then imagine voices calling out "loser" or "faggot." I grab it from her fingers, roll my eyes, bring it to my mouth and take a hit.

I think back to all those parties I never went to when I could have and I take another hit. I think back to all the quiet nights by myself and I take another. I think back to my daily routine of sleep, school, home, sleep, and take one final drag.

I cough out all the smoke. I feel my throat burn. I feel my lungs collapse for a second. I feel free and alive.

"You okay?" Ella asks. She pats my back.

"I'm fine."

She nods. "I got some good stuff from that old cashier at Food Basics down by Meadowgrove."

"She deals?" I say.

"Shocking, right? I babysat her grandkids last week for two grams."

I shake my head, smile, and laugh between more coughing fits. I feel my eyes tear up and burn.

We continue passing the joint back and forth. I take in more smoke each time and try to blow out rings. When the joint burns out, we decide to call it a night.

"You have my number in case anything happens," she says. "Try not to think or worry too much… paranoia can be a bitch."

"I'll be all right," I tell her.

"You sure?" she asks.

"Yeah. I feel perfect."

She reaches over, gives me a hug and heads toward the path leading downhill. I stay seated on the picnic table.

I watch the road for a bit and, again, count the cars that pass by. After a few minutes, I jump off the picnic table, and roll on the ground. After a while, I get up, watching each step I take. I notice the detail in every sway of grass blades, each swing of naked tree branches, the movement of my arms as they flop around my sides like noodles.

Everything moves like a stop-motion animated film. I notice the slight pauses between each twitch and each change in motion. I reach the base of the hill.

I look up and for the first time I notice how bright the stars are.

Modern Beatniks
Jill Kennedy

I balance Kevin's bike and a bag filled with booze as we wait for his friend Joel to meet us in front of his apartment on Eglinton Avenue, just west of Bathurst.

Kevin and I took his bikes out to Centre Island and cruised around for the day. Tonight will involve getting drunk and checking out the NXNE Festival. It is our second date.

"Hey man, I'm downstairs," Kevin says into his phone. He is nervous as he looks down at me with boyish blue eyes and moves them over to the hard, metal door in front of us. Kevin rubs beads of sweat off his forehead with the back of his hand and runs the same hand through his dirty blonde hair.

Joel, a stick of a man, eases the door open. He is shirtless and barely holding onto a short, fat glass of brown liquid.

"Into your Wild Turkey, I see," says Kevin.

"Every day," says Joel, monotone.

"Can you put down the bourbon and help us carry this

stuff, man?" says Kevin.

"Yeah, I'll bring up a bike."

"I don't mind taking the bike," I say.

Joel sighs. "I go-o-o-t it. Just hold this." He hands me his glass.

I take a whiff and frown. I pull the brown paperbag of booze closer to me and amble up two flights of stairs to Joel's apartment.

Joel lives in apartment two but spends most of his time down the hall at apartment four where his ex-girlfriend Sarah lives. They dated for a while but she moved back home and he took over. She still pays rent. Kevin and I are staying in Joel's room tonight while he passes out in apartment four.

"Let's go to Sarah's place," says Joel.

"Sure," Kevin and I say.

I retrieve a bottle of Georges Duboeuf from my bag. We proceed down the hall.

"You're drinking wine?" Joel asks.

I nod and hand him the bottle.

"Oh, Beaujolais. Good choice," Joel says. He sets the bottle down on the countertop. He opens up a cupboard and some drawers and retrieves a wine glass and a corkscrew. Joel twists the screw into the cork and with a *clunk*, the bottle is open.

"Wow, you're a natural," I say.

"I've opened many fancy wine bottles before. Used to

work at Auberge du Pommier as a server but I got fired for telling my boss he was a pompous asshole."

※

It's 3 a.m. Kevin and I arrive back from Last Temptation, a hipster bar in Kensington Market. He ordered us a pitcher of red wine sangria. Prior to that, we watched the band The National play a show in front of hundreds of people at Dundas Square.

Kevin and I stumble up the stairs into Joel's room, strip down, and fall into his bed.

"What a great day," says Kevin.

"I enjoyed it. Thanks for everything," I say.

"Yeah, it was nice of Joel to let us stay here."

"I hope he didn't mind too much. He's really cool."

"I want to be in his frame of mind," Kevin says and stares at the ceiling.

I roll over and face him. "What do you mean?"

"It's like he's achieved something... reached some sort of state. I think it has something to do with his vegetarian, alternative lifestyle."

"He lives like a true artist," I say.

Kevin stands up and picks his rugged jean shorts off the hardwood floor. He wrestles with them until a pack of cigarettes and a lighter slide into his hand. He walks over to the window and lights up a Belmont. I get up from the bed and join him at the windowsill. We share the smoke and the view of a taller, windowless building across the street.

"That building is weird," I say. "You could die drunk in there and no one would ever know."

Kevin stares ahead. "I think I want to move in with Joel."

"But he has a roommate," I say.

"Joel doesn't care for Davis. I mean, you've seen apartment two. Joel wants to move into four once Sarah and her shitty roommate move out."

I blink. "Yeah," I say. "Davis is gross…What's it like to live up here price-wise?"

"It's fairly cheap once you go north of the Bloor subway line. I think it's less than $550 for each of us."

We stare out the window. Joel's journal is lodged behind the windowpane and the window screen. I look for too long and scan the last line. It reads: "And I think you're a parasite."

I turn away and eye his desk. It hosts a pastel-blue Smith-Corona typewriter and a stack of American literature: Bukowski, Kerouac, Fitzgerald, Hunter S. Thompson. A copy of Camus' The Outsider rests on top. Joel belongs right there with these tragic, drunk, starving writers and beatniks.

I look back at Kevin. He sits, naked, in a folding chair

with a small fan in his lap. He ashes his Belmont in an empty bottle of Boneshaker IPA. It sizzles. We move back into bed and crawl under crimson sheets.

If Kevin is moving in with Joel, I imagine I will never see him again. As a suburban resident, I don't see why he'd even bother asking me to hang out when he lives north of the city.

❧

Kevin and I have been drunk all day. He took me on a date to the Jays game. We drank before, during and after the game.

"Joel says we can stay over again," says Kevin.

"I guess this means another drunken evening?"

"Definitely."

We hop on the subway to Joel's place.

After a few hours of lounging and listening to vinyl records, I receive a text from my friend Heather, who lives a subway stop north of Joel's. Kevin, Joel and I agree that she should join us.

While we wait for Heather, I stare at four drinks and wonder what to choose: a Somersby cider, a DAB beer, a Blackthorn Cider and/or a Rekorderlig Wild Berry Cider.

Heather arrives and I introduce everyone. Heather and I catch up for a bit while Kevin and Joel take turns choosing songs.

A live version of a song starts playing. Two seconds in, I ask, "What is this?"

Joel turns around slowly and glares at me.

I blink. Ah, shit. It's Radiohead. Fuck. If I want to continue dating Kevin and impressing Joel, I need to step up my game and listen to more Radiohead.

Joel looks back at the record player.

"'Idioteque' is my favourite song," says Heather.

Everyone nods.

"I listened to it walking home in the snow once and it was really scary," she says.

"Have you ever listened to 'Idioteque' while wanting to kill yourself?" says Joel.

"Probably," says Kevin.

Heather and I look at each other.

I'm drunk enough to express my concern.

"Well, dude, I hope you aren't actually suicidal," I say.

"Psh, I wanna be dead by thirty," says Joel, chugging his beer. He shrugs his way into the kitchen and pours a glass of Wild Turkey.

Kevin bobs his head to Fidlar's song, "Cheap Beer."

"But why?" I ask. "You have so much potential. You've already released a CD and you can write amazingly."

"Well," Joel declares, "I'm going to be my fucked-up, barely functional self and try and write good music and just take what shows up. I'm not happy. I'm full-blown fuckin' facedown depressed."

I blink and ease my beer closer to my face. I take a slow sip.

Kevin chimes in. "He doesn't want to die because he is suicidal. It's much more of a choice than that."

Joel raises his fresh glass of bourbon and takes a swig.

❦

The rest of the evening blurs past me.

Heather leaves after two hours. Joel swears. He thought he would get laid. Kevin passes out sitting up on Joel's couch listening to a Devo record.

I check my phone. I open a text from Heather. It says: "Joel is an ass!! I'm glad I left, girl. I don't know why you thought he was so cool! He's just like every other city kid. I like Kevin though. He's a cutie. Keep it up girl!!!" I put down my phone and try not to laugh.

Joel and I decide to go outside and smoke. We drag our backs down the wall until we are sitting on the concrete, our legs stretched out. We talk and talk about how impossible relationships are, and how I like Kevin too much.

"I don't think he likes me," I say.

"You're cool, Jill. You're cooler than anyone he's ever dated," Joel says and drags on his cigarette.

For some reason, validation from Joel wipes out all of the embarrassing actions I brought forth earlier in the night. I make a mental note to listen to Radiohead's album *Kid A* as soon as I get back home.

"The thing is, I don't think it'll go anywhere, man," I say. "I feel like I annoy him. I just wish I could have something consistent…stable, even."

"Ugh, fuck stability," Joel cuts in. "I felt something genuine for a girl a long time ago and it was the most surreal thing. I felt I could live the rest of my life like that. It disappeared. A few months went by and I've felt like a tin can for a couple years. But that's enough honesty for now."

Joel drops his cigarette on the ground beside him. He hops up and twists his foot against the burning cigarette until it goes out.

"With Kevin," says Joel, "he's a different kind of fucked up. You just have to realize he's one part dumb, one part rational, one part reckless and one part angry. I hope things work out between you two but it's hard to get into his brain."

"Thanks, man. I'm glad we could talk about this," I say.

"We have good conversations." Joel unlocks the front door of the apartment and holds it open for me.

He and I head back upstairs and drag Kevin into Sarah's apartment and onto a mattress on the floor. The empty room echoes at us as Kevin hits the mattress. Then

I do. The hot air makes my skin sticky and uncomfortable. Kevin rolls away from me and falls asleep. I stare at the ceiling for hours.

Belmonts and Carnations
Samantha Ashenhurst

I haven't seen Mark since my birthday—the day I figured out that he's been seeing his co-worker Vicki behind my back. I had long suspected it, but I didn't know for sure until I read his text messages while he slept on my couch.

He denies everything, insisting that there's nothing between him and Vicki beyond a close friendship. He laughs off my suspicions, calling me crazy and irrational, insisting that doubting him is selfish. I don't believe him. His story has gaps, unanswered questions, blatant half-truths and strategic omissions.

Despite his lies, I feel an obligation to Mark. I know things between us are over; it's only a matter of time before one of us bothers to say it.

We haven't avoided each other intentionally. We simply haven't made the time to see each other for the entire month of May. We still speak on the phone daily. We've reconciled as best as a couple that has been together for three years—and, in a way, still love each other—can.

I can't figure out why Mark won't just break up with me or, at the very least, confess to cheating so I can end things with him. Maybe he feels that whatever we have might be worth fixing, or maybe he just doesn't have the energy to initiate the break-up conversation.

As the spring sun warms my face, I drop my smoke on the damp cement outside Wellesley Subway Station, grinding the butt with my toe. Two months ago, as my suspicions about Mark grew, I started to purchase king-sized packs of Belmonts from the newspaper stand at Islington Station on my way home from his place.

I smoke in secret—alone, hidden around corners or in alleyways, in unfamiliar neighbourhoods, out of sight of anyone who may recognize me and brand me a "smoker." I haven't told Mark. Instead, I waited for the inevitable confrontation, when he would find a pack in my purse or smell the unmistakable aroma on my fingers or in my hair. But he's never mentioned it. I wonder if he's even noticed.

I walk into the station and pay my fare at the turnstile. I pause before walking down the stairs toward the tracks of the Northbound subway to the Bloor-Yonge Station. I retrieve my phone from my purse. The time on the screen glows 5:50. Mark starts his bartending shift at O'Grady's up the block at 6:00.

He got the job at the pub three months ago—around the same time I landed my college internship. After three years of living in different cities, we felt elated by the idea of working a block from each other. We stayed up late on the phone, filling the gaps between the "I love yous" and the "I miss yous" with talk about how this was the best thing to happen to us, about the pos-sibility of me getting a job after the internship, about how we could finally live together downtown—but things changed.

I decide to wait around to see Mark before he starts work. After all, he is my boyfriend.

I spot Mark coming up the stairs before he sees me. He wears the same black jeans, the same small knapsack slung over his right shoulder, but something's weird—he looks different. Thinner. Paler. Oversized headphones hide half of his face. He holds his Discman, a gift from my parents last Christmas, in his hands.

"Hey," I say, waving as I approach him.

"Oh, hi," he says, avoiding my eyes as he removes his headphones with a crooked smile.

We stand a foot away from each other. He looks unfamiliar to me now. A black hat, the kind made popular by Che Guevara, covers his greasy black hair. Patchy black stubble pokes out from above his lip and across his chin, evidence that he hasn't shaved in two days. His thin face appears more gaunt than usual.

"Um," I mutter, my eyes darting around the station, looking anywhere but his eyes. "You start work at six, I guess?"

"Yeah," he says, looking down at his clunky shoes. "And you just finished?"

"Yeah."

We stand facing each other, but not looking at each other. I make eye contact with an old woman standing near the stairs, with a bouquet of pink and yellow carnations gripped between her wrinkled hands. I recognize her long silver hair pulled back into a loose bun and bundled with a floral scarf. She and her husband run the newspaper stand at Islington where I buy my smokes.

"Well," Mark says with a shrug, "I'd better get to work if I want to be on time."

"Yeah," I nod, my hands tucked into the back pockets of my blue jeans. "We should get together," I add.

We hug, crisscrossed, like distant relatives. Our bodies, out of practice with one another, bump together and we both apologize.

I look at the elderly woman, still clutching her flowers, as Mark and I hug. She catches my eyes and smiles, and I return one, wondering who she thinks Mark is to me.

My cousin? My friend? My brother?

I realize that I don't even know who Mark is to me.

We separate, and he walks toward the doors that will take him outside. I walk down the stairs and stand on the platform.

The subway pulls into the station, blasting my face with warm air and pushing my hair in multiple directions.

I board the train and take a seat by the window. I wait for the train to pull out, to take me away from Toronto, away from Mark, and away from Vicki.

Rare Cards
Rob Redford

All the lights in the house were out and everybody slept but me.

I was still awake, watching my small, dimly lit TV with the volume one green bar above mute. I didn't want anybody to know I was up and watching the kinds of adult-themed shows that only played after one in the morning. I sat on the floor with my ear close to the speaker, watching the shows so I could teach my fellow fifth-graders about girls and sex, and about what's "normal" and what's "weird," during our recess talks.

The TV flickered and a chilling sound echoed towards me from another room.

I rose from the floor, confused, hearing a series of howls and whimpers. I trudged across my room and opened the door, staring down the dark hallway past my sister's room on the left and the bathroom to the right. The sounds came from my mother's bedroom.

I wondered whether or not to approach Mom's room.

The noise almost sounded like the show I was watching, but they frightened me. I wished the cries would stop, but they continued; a long, low-pitched bawl preceded a short, shrill howl, one following the other, again and again.

My eyes stung as I started to drift towards her bedroom door. I dotted the hallway floor with my falling tears.

I knocked on Mom's door.

"Are you okay?" I asked as I entered her room.

Silence lingered before she replied with a weak "I'm fine."

Darkness prevented me from seeing more than the outline of her body on the bed and the movement of her hand sweeping across her face.

"What's wrong?" I asked.

"N— ...nothing," she choked back.

I closed the door and sulked back to my room, the back of my hand wiping away my tears. I was no longer in the mood to watch sultry TV shows. I turned off the TV, threw myself facedown onto my bed and cried until I fell asleep. I wondered if my sister Alex had also heard Mom, and I thought that, maybe, we were all still awake.

The next morning I walked to school with Alex, who was older than me by two years. Neither of us saw Mom before we left and we assumed that she was still asleep. I didn't ask Alex if she had heard Mom's cries—we simply spent the eight-minute walk along the Glen Erin Trail quoting funny lines from TV shows.

"You'll have to speak up. I'm wearing a towel," said Alex, quoting Homer Simpson.

Green trees and the fences separating us from the backyards of houses flanked the wide concrete path we walked. We herded with dozens of other students toward our elementary school.

After school, I walked home with my friends through the forest shortcut. We bought candy at the convenience store before splitting up.

When I arrived home, my grandparents stood at the door to greet me instead of Mom. Granddad gave me his signature smile before telling me that Mom had gone to the hospital earlier in the day. Alex sat on the old black couch with her head down and her shoes on.

"Why is Mom in the hospital?" I asked.

Granddad replied with a long silence and a solemn expression.

"Your mom wasn't feeling well today," said Grandma, leaning forward. "So she had to go to the hospital to feel better."

"Okay..." I threw my backpack on the couch beside

Alex and led the way to the car.

At the hospital, we took the elevator to the top floor and entered a small, dark room occupied by my mom and one other patient, who slept on the bed closest to the door. They were separated by a single faded blue curtain. The roommate's bedside table was cluttered with small toys and plastic trinkets. We hurried past her and reached Mom's bed.

Mom's long brown hair looked thin and unwashed, and her eyes looked heavy, which contrasted sharply with the smile that she gave us.

"What a view from up here," Granddad said, looking out the window.

"How's your roommate?" asked Grandma.

I looked out the window as they talked, staring at the dark blue sky surrounding the heavy, urban Toronto blocks.

"She's really nice. She gave me these Pokémon cards," said Mom, pointing to her bedside table.

"Anything rare?" I said as I turned around.

My eyes, searching for the cards, locked on the marks that lined the inside of my mother's arms. Dark red gashes ran horizontally across her wrists, already starting to scab over.

"What happened to your arms?" I managed to ask.

My grandparents excused themselves to get some coffee. Mom looked at Alex and me with calm eyes that drooped under her sedation.

She explained what had happened during the previous night. Mom was always transparent when she talked to us. She never wanted to prevent us from knowing the truth. Her candid admission that she had cut her own arms with a knife made my sister cry.

"I had to come to the hospital," Mom said. "I was so depressed that I wanted to kill myself." She closed her eyes and added, "I'm so sorry."

I was surprised at how numb I felt. I tried to take in the information. My body was still as my gaze remained fixed on the view outside the window. My mom had been depressed in the past, but as far as I knew, she had never done anything like this. Alex hurried to hug my mom, breathing deeply and sobbing heavily into her hospital gown.

I turned and hugged Mom as well. I asked her if she was still feeling sad and she told us that she felt much better. She told us that the doctors gave her medicine, that she would have to stay in the hospital for a few days, and that Grandma and Granddad would stay at our place to take care of us. Her smile reassured me that she was feeling better.

"Why would they put you on the top floor?" I asked.

"This is the psych ward," Mom replied. "It's where they put all the crazy people."

"You're not crazy!" said Alex, wiping her wet face with

her baggy sweater.

"I know," said my mom, as she petted Alex's head.

She turned and looked at me.

"I'm sick, but in a different way than you're used to. I'm just a little sick in my brain—but I promise that I'm going to be okay. Okay?" she said.

Alex sniffled and squeezed my mom harder as I thought about all that I had just learned.

Before we left, Mom gave my sister and me a Pokémon card. I looked down at mine and saw a smiling purple rat named "Ratatat."

❀

The next day, my grandparents drove me and Alex to school.

At recess, I sat on the grass with my best friend, Matthew. We shared nearly everything with each other, so I didn't hesitate to tell him what happened to my mom.

"I've never heard of someone going to the hospital for being sad," he said. I could tell that he didn't understand.

"She's sick, man. Only she's sick in her brain," I told him as I pointed to my head. "It's, like, she just has to use a different kind of medicine, y'know?"

"That's kind of weird," he said.

"Kind of," I replied. "There was an entire floor in the

hospital for people who are sick like that. So it's kind of normal."

"I guess so," said Matthew.

I thought to myself about how I have another thing to teach my classmates.

The Pipe
Mathew Spadafora

"Do you want to watch *Austin Powers*, Josh?"
"I don't want to watch that movie. It's fucking stupid."

Mom doesn't let me swear, especially not around my sister, Alex. The word "fuck" makes me uncomfortable, but it sounds kinda cool when my older cousin Josh says it.

He sits on the floor, absorbed by the Gameboy in his hands—my Gameboy, my Pokémon game.

"My mom rented *Austin Powers* for us," I say. "I wanna watch it."

"Shut up! Jesus!" Josh looks up from the game and scowls at me. "I don't even know why I still have sleepovers with you. You're a whiny fucking baby."

Mom walks into to the living room. She carries a bag of salt and vinegar chips.

"Hey boys," she says. "What're you up to?"

"Nothing, Aunt Helen!" Josh jumps up and throws my Gameboy to the floor. "I was just showing Matt how to beat his Pokémon game, then we were gonna watch the movie you got for us."

Mom smiles.

"The sun's still out. Why don't you go play at the park?" she says as she pulls the bag of chips open with a pop and hands it to Josh. He takes a handful of chips. I shift in my seat on the couch.

"Matt? Would you want to go to the park?" asks Mom.

"I guess so."

"Good idea, Aunt Helen," Josh says. He sucks in air between mouthfuls of chips. Mom smiles again and leaves the room.

Crumbs fall to the carpet. Josh wipes his greasy hands over his gut and across his Diesel T-shirt and throws the bag to the floor. It falls beside my Gameboy.

"Can we go to that cool pipe?" he says.

"Mom said we should go to the park," I reply.

"The park is for losers."

"Mom said—" I begin, but he interrupts me.

"Shut up, you retard. We're going to the pipe."

Duncaster Drive, the street I've lived on since I was four, trails up on a slope through the Brant Hills area. Just up the street from my house is the Duncaster Ravine. Duncaster Drive winds through the middle of the forest. On one side of the road, a set of stairs leads down to a winding trail through the small ravine behind my elementary school. On the other side, the water from a small waterfall runs under the road through a large pipe and continues flowing through the ravine. The older kids at St. Mark's Elementary School boast at recess about walking through the pipe. Teenagers go there at night to do drugs and write graffiti.

I follow Josh out into the foyer.

"This time," he says, "we're going through it. Don't you dare chicken out."

He grabs his shoes from the mat by the door. His big fingers fumble with the laces. His feet are twice as big as mine.

"I don't really want to get my shoes wet," I say. "Mom bought me new Nike sneakers last month for my tenth birthday."

I look at my new sneakers by the door.

Josh scowls again. He turns from the front door toward the kitchen. He nudges me when he passes. His shoes make a trail of mud over the hardwood of the hallway.

He returns a few seconds later from the kitchen with a fistful of plastic bags.

"If you don't want your stupid shoes to get wet, wear plastic bags over them. Now, come on. Maybe I'll actually enjoy my time here if you grow a pair and follow me."

He throws the bags at me. They catch the air and float to my feet.

49

❊

I stand on the sidewalk. Josh teeters on rocks around the waterfall. The brown water splashes on the rocks. The rain from last night's downpour makes the waterfall overflow.

"I'm not going to wait around for you all day, Matt."

He climbs down the rocks toward the mouth of the pipe. The water rushes over his shoes.

"Seriously, I'm walking through it," he says. "Catch ya later, loser."

His head disappears from view.

I walk down from the road to the edge of the waterfall. I look into the pipe. Josh stands with his legs spread over the rush of water and shuffles forward along the rounded sides of the pipe. He stretches his arms out for balance. His fingers only graze the walls.

Josh calls back. "It's easy," he says, "Even someone like you can do it!"

He laughs.

I step onto a rock in the water. A path of stepping-stones stretches out in front of me toward to the mouth of the pipe. Brown water sloshes up against my sneakers. I jump backward onto the grass.

Josh's voice echoes from inside the pipe.

"Put the plastic bags on your feet, you pussy!"

I pull bunches of bags from my pocket. I fall back onto the grass and reach down to my feet to cover them with the plastic. I knot the handles of the bags around my ankles.

"I'm coming, Josh," I call out. My voice shakes.

I step back onto the same rock I stood on before. My right foot slips from under me but I catch my balance as I wave my arms. *I'm glad Josh isn't watching me*, I think.

I take another step. My foot slips again. I fall hard into the brown water. The water soaks my jeans and t-shirt. My head falls under the torrent. I snap back up and gasp for air. The plastic bags fall off of my feet and flow with the water into the pipe.

Water fills my sneakers.

Josh roars with laughter from the road above.

I cry. He can't tell. My face drips with dirty water.

He pulls his bulky flip phone out from his pocket and points the camera flash at me.

"This— is—fucking—amazing!" he says.

I stand up from the water and walk up the slope toward Josh. My wet hair lies flat against my forehead and my clothes feel heavy. My wet shoes slip on the grass as I climb.

"I'll… I'll tell Mom you made me do it," I manage to say between heaves. "I didn't want to… it was your idea…"

"You're going to get in so much trouble," he jeers. "I wanted to go to the park the whole time. But you wouldn't let me!"

I squeeze water from my shorts and the water dribbles down into my new sneakers, now soaked in water from the pipe.

Trip to the Taj
Jai Sangha

"We won't make it in time," my dad says from the backseat. "Just turn around. That way we'll beat the evening traffic going into Delhi."

"Oh, you shut up," Mom says in her calm tone.

Robby, my younger brother, cranks the volume to turn up the music. I manoeuvre the Skoda around a cow lazing in the middle of the road. It chews on green shoots. I press on the accelerator and the speed dial rises above a hundred and twenty. We are only a few kilometres away.

"You were going to hit that cow," says dad. "Drive slower. Otherwise it would be a sad ending to a sad day."

I keep driving, the orange needle pointing at a hundred and twenty five. I feel the cool air from the air conditioning vents that have been running at full blast since we left Delhi.

We finally turn off of the main highway, in the midst of rickshaws, bicycles, trucks and stray dogs, onto the road that leads to the Taj Mahal. The Yamuna River, or what remains of it besides from foam and litter, flows beside the road. A huge red brick fort emerges from behind the lush green trees on our right.

"This must be the Red Fort. This is where Shah Jahan was imprisoned and looked at the Taj Mahal towards the end of his life," I say, recalling high school history lessons about the Mughal times in India.

"And that is the window, the one between the two white pillars, from where he used to see the Taj Mahal," my dad declares.

"Dad, there is no way you know that. Most windows here have two pillars on either side," I say.

"Son, I am telling you that's the one."

Robby looks at me and rolls his eyes behind his glasses. I stay quiet.

"Ma, can you pass the camcorder to Robby? It's in the outer pocket of my backpack," I ask.

"The view isn't very nice. If we had more time we could've stopped to see the Red Fort," my dad says as he passes the camcorder to my brother.

I pull left into the parking lot for the Taj Mahal. The barrier on the road reads "NO CARS BEYOND THIS POINT." I roll down the window to get the parking permit from a salt-and-pepper-bearded man holding a roll of white ticket paper. The smell of sweat and manure hits my nostrils.

"Parking kitna hai?" I ask in Hindi, which means, "How much is the parking?"

"Seventy-five rupees, sir."

"But the board outside says fifty rupees."

"That's an old board, sir. Those are old rates. They have changed now," he says.

"Where are the new rates written?" I put the car into gear.

"Okay, sir, fifty is okay," he says. I hand him the crinkled Gandhi bills that Robby passes to me.

Two camels pull bright red carts and cross in front of us. I reverse into the faded white lines. Three men dressed in black shirts and trousers approach us. One holds an SLR camera. I take out my camera bag and strap it around my neck. The man with the camera moves towards my dad on the other side of the car. Another man blocks my way.

"Sir, do you need a guide? Sir, total history of Taj Mahal, sir."

I look back at my mom, who shakes her head.

"No, we are fine, thank you," I say.

"But, sir, A to Z story of Taj Mahal. And I will give you a discount."

"Mere bhai," I say, using the Hindi words for "my brother." "We don't need a guide. We are fine. Why don't you look for someone else who might want a guide?"

I push gently by him and wait for my mom to come. The guide moves towards my dad. The man my dad was talking to now drives a motorized rickshaw silently towards us.

"Please, sir, come on. Ready to go," he says in English with a thick Indian accent. We all climb on.

"Sir, I will first take you to Meena Bazaar. It has the best saris and blankets. They are world-famous, sir."

I look at my watch. It is 4:05.

"But the website says that the Taj Mahal closes at five in the evening. Just go there," I say in Hindi.

"The what, sir?"

"Internet," I seethe.

"Oh, no sir, that is the old timings. It is open till seven now," he says without looking back. He turns left off of the road full of pedestrians, rickshaws and camel-carts towards small shops beside an empty fountain. The electric motor buzzes to a halt.

"Sir, come this way."

The driver leads us into one of the shops with drapes and colourful saris hanging through the window. My family and I sit on the leather cushion bench. The white ceiling fan rotates at full speed above us. A bald shopkeeper pulls out a black sari with white paisley patterns on it. The other shopkeeper walks out with the rickshaw driver. My mom holds the sari.

"This is A-1 quality, ma'am. This sari is made from banana peels. It doesn't shrink and it keeps you warm in cold weather and cold in warm weather. It is very unique material." The shopkeeper pulls out a red sari from the rack.

"This is going to be a while. I'm stepping out," I tell Robby.

I walk to the fountain and look at the green algae stuck to the floor of the bowl. I see the shopkeeper and the rickshaw driver standing under a tree. The shopkeeper hands the driver some rupee bills.

Of course. I check my watch again. I look beyond the trees and try to see how far the Taj Mahal was from where we were. It is the last day of my summer break before I fly back to Toronto for the fall semester.

"No, no, we don't want anything," I hear my dad say as he walks out of the door and holds it open for my mom and Robby. The shopkeeper pleads for them to stay and look at another "export-quality" piece. My dad walks towards me.

"Bete (son), where's the driver? Call him and let's go."

I wave to the driver and he quickly walks towards the rickshaw and waits.

"Sir, did not like anything, sir? I will take you another shop. Very good kurtas."

"Go straight to the Taj Mahal," my dad says. "Or we are not paying you anything."

It is 4:35pm. We walk to the two line-ups formed in front of the ticket counter outside tall brown brick walls that form the last barrier before for the Taj Mahal. The "Ladies" line is a lot shorter than the "Gentlemen" line at the booth.

My mom and dad stand in their respective lines. I stay back with Robby. My mom reaches the booth first and signals my dad to walk over to purchase tickets for the whole family. I see my dad get to the booth and shake his head. I walk closer to see what is going on.

"She has an Indian driver's licence with her. How can you say she is a foreigner?" my dad says to the man behind the counter.

"She looks like a foreigner. We have to charge her seven hundred fifty rupees," the man says in Hindi.

"She lives in Punjab," my dad says. "Here is her licence with the address on it. We are both doctors. I am not paying anything more than the twenty rupees you are charging the rest of us."

The man calls a colleague over, mumbles something in Hindi, and points first at my mom's licence, then at her. They both look at my light-complexioned mother.

"Sir, she looks like she is a foreigner," the second man says.

My dad puts down a total of eighty rupees on the counter.

"She is an Indian resident, and that is all I am paying," he says as he slides the money towards the man.

The man looks at the licence and slowly hands it back. He grabs the money and gives back four ticket stubs.

"Please, hurry to the entrance. The gates close at five,"

says the man and he points to the arch entrance of the outer walls of the Taj Mahal.

We all walk towards the metal detectors under the arch, screen through without any problems, and make our way to the doors of the Taj Mahal courtyard.

A kit of pigeons flies low over the gardens, perches on top of the doors, and flaps its wings. The grand white marble structure stands in front of us.

We see the Taj.

Lemon Meringue Pie
Laura Gillis

I stand in my grandparents' garden at the front of their house. The sky is clear, allowing the hot California sun to beat down on my pale, freckled skin. A cool sea breeze rushes through the air, sweeping my hair across my face. I tuck my hair behind my ears and step under my grandparents four-foot-tall lemon tree to shade myself from the sun.

Grammy says I need to pick six lemons so we can make her lemon meringue pie together. I count five bright yellow dimpled skin lemons in the wooden basket I grasp in my hand.

I spot the perfect lemon at the top of the tree. I stand on my tippy toes and reach to touch it. I split it from the branch and place it in the basket with the other lemons.

I skip from the garden through the gates and onto the front porch. Grammy sits on a metal lawn chair. Her legs are crossed and she reaches her hand up to her mouth to take a drag of her cigarette. She presses it on the ashtray on the table beside her and it sizzles out.

"Have you picked six lemons, my dear?" she asks.

"Yup, see!" I shove the basket in her face.

Grammy takes the basket from my hands and inspects the lemons.

"These lemons are perfect, Laura. Let's go to the kitchen and start making the pie," she says, smiling and showing all of her teeth. She stands up and walks into the small, one-storey house.

I follow her into the kitchen, pushing open the saloon-style doors and pretending that I'm a cowgirl. I sit down at the glass kitchen table, waiting for Grammy to pull out all of the ingredients.

I admire her as she bustles around the kitchen. A quilted apron drapes across her stomach, covering her purple dress pants and white short-sleeved dress shirt. A pink breast cancer ribbon is pinned to her shirt's collar. Beads of sweat form on her forehead. Her thick-rimmed glasses slide down her large, arched nose. She uses her index finger to push them back into place. Her curly white hair is frizzy from the heat and humidity.

"Are you ready, dear?" she turns to ask me. I jump out of my seat, glide towards the counter and study the ingredients that are lined up to the left of the sink. She places a big blue bowl in front of me and hands me an egg.

"Crack this egg into the bowl," she orders. I pound the egg on the side of the bowl and crush the inside of the egg and the shell together.

"Oops, I'm sorry." I look up at Grammy. She giggles softly at my clumsiness.

"That's okay. We have plenty of eggs," she says, pulling another one out of the carton. "Let's try this again." She places the egg in my hand and puts her hand on top of mine. Her hand guides mine to lightly tap the egg on the side of the bowl, cracking it perfectly. I pour flour into the bowl and stir it together with the egg.

"Can you do the rest, Grammy? I'm getting tired," I say.

"Of course, dear," she says, picking me up so I can sit on the counter. "You can watch instead. You should learn how to bake though; men love a woman who knows how to bake."

"But I'm only eight years old!" I exclaim.

"Well, you have plenty of time to learn, then," she says with a giggle.

"How have you been feeling lately, Grammy?"

"Sorry, what did you say, dear?" She reaches towards her ear to turn up the volume on her hearing aid.

"I said, how are you feeling since you got out of the hospital?"

Her blue eyes peek through her glasses. She stops stirring the batter and turns to look at me.

"I feel much better now, Laura. The breast cancer took a lot of my strength, but I've been resting a lot and I feel like I'm getting back to normal. Don't worry about me, though. I'm strong and I'm fighting through it. Today is actually my first day back in the kitchen and I get the pleasure of baking with you," she says, kissing my forehead. I smile.

I gaze out the window that's over the kitchen sink. A hummingbird drinks from the water fountain that stands in the middle of their front porch. Its wings flap quickly as it buzzes around the fountain. Hummingbirds are Grammy's favourite birds.

I look over at Grammy. I watch her float around the kitchen as she finishes the pie. She radiates grace as she adds the rest of the ingredients into the bowl. She doesn't make a mistake. She uses a spatula to scrape the batter into a pie pan and slides the pie into the oven.

"Twenty minutes until the pie is ready!" she says, setting the egg timer.

She sits down at the glass kitchen table and wipes her forehead with a napkin. I jump off the counter and climb onto the chair beside her. She wraps her arms around me and squeezes me. I inhale an aroma of lemons and cigarettes.

"I used to bake with my grandma all the time when I was your age. That was a long time ago. I'll be eighty years old soon. Gosh, I'm a dinosaur," she snickers.

"I love spending time with you, Grammy," I say. "I don't want to go home to Toronto tomorrow."

"I'll tell your Dad to bring you back soon. Next time

we can make cherry cheesecake, okay?"

"Okay," I say as my stomach growls. "How much longer until the pie is ready?"

"Eighteen minutes, dear."

I rest my head on Grammy's shoulder, close my eyes, and breathe in the aroma of lemon meringue pie.

Pop Bottle
Dylan Smart

"Hey, Pop Bottle! You steal my fucking lighter?" Dad barks as he blasts through the back door of our modest bungalow and stomps out onto the deck. An unlit cigarette dances on his lips.

"No! I told you, mahn," Keith says. "You probably left it on your work bench in the garage. It's probably lost in all that rubble."

Dad glares at Keith through his knockoff Oakley sunglasses.

"Bullshit. Check your pockets."

Keith stands up from his seat around the glass patio table holding half a two-four of empty Coors Lite bottles, a crowded ash tray and a Tupperware container full of watermelon rinds.

Keith is one of Dad's longtime friends—the partier type. Dad calls him "Pop Bottle" because his bifocals are as thick as the pop bottles they used to make out of glass. Keith lived with us fourteen years ago after he lost his licence for drinking and driving and helped with taking care of my younger brother Dalton, who was less than a year old at the time. Keith wore a cast on his wrist from the accident and let me doodle on it with a permanent marker. I doodled so much that I ran out of white space.

Keith now stabs his hands into the pockets of his cargo shorts, fiddles around for a mo-ment, and then stops. He pulls an orange Bic lighter from his pocket with a puzzled look across his face.

"You're an idiot," Dad says and rips the lighter from Keith's hand. Dad smirks, sits down at the table beside Dan, our neighbour, and lights his cigarette.

"This bastard's constantly stealing my lighters!" Dad says as he points his unopened beer bottle towards Keith. Dan smirks and shakes his head.

"I swear, he's like those hawks that hover over these farm fields," continues Dad, point-ing the same unopened beer bottle at the expanding fields around us. "As soon as he spots a lighter, he swoops down and snatches it!"

Keith snickers and sits back into his chair.

Dad twists off the cap and tosses it onto the table. The cap clinks as it lands.

"The only difference is"—Dad takes a swig of beer—"those hawks can see for miles and you can't see worth shit!"

Dad turns in his seat towards the rusty thermometer mounted to the brick wall of the house. His beer belly squishes against the armrest.

"Ninety degrees!" He swivels further in his chair until he faces me and stops. "Are your buddies coming over to swim, Dyl? Pool's eighty-five!"

I close the lid on the smoking barbeque and turn towards Dad.

"Nah, nobody's free. It's just me tonight."

Keith pulls a pack of Players Light cigarettes out of the breast pocket of his faded yellow, button-down T-shirt. It hangs loosely over his skinny torso. He stashes the cigarette between his lips and reaches for the orange Bic on the table. Dad swipes the lighter before Keith reaches it.

"Oh c'mon, mahn!" Keith says.

"No way!" says Dad.

Dan fishes in the pockets of his swimming trunks and pulls out a stainless steel Zippo, and tosses it to Keith.

"Here, use mine, Keith. But if you pocket that one, I'll come for you."

"Slimy bastard," Dad mumbles.

Keith lights his cigarette and takes a long drag. He cranes his neck towards the sky and exhales.

※

One night, back when Keith lived with us, Dad, Dalton, Keith and I watched *Spider-Man* in the upstairs living room. During the movie, Keith stood up from his spot beside me on the loveseat and snuck out the front door. Dad was asleep and didn't notice. The movie ended by the time Keith rattled the door open and came back inside. Dad woke up.

"Where the hell did you go?" Dad asked.

"The trampoline—that thing's a blast!" Keith said between heavy breaths.

Dad raised his voice. "Bullshit. What the hell were you doing out there?"

"I'm tellin' you, mahn, I was jumping on the trampoline. I was getting kooked up in here and I wanted to get some fresh air."

Dad glares at Keith with a look I have never seen.

"I had one condition, Keith," he says.

❦

I open the barbeque lid and adjust the sausages with the tongs. Flames reach up through the grill and the hot smoke burns my eyes. I sweep the lid down and press my forearm against my eyelids.

"So, Dylan," Keith says. "You're all into the fitness stuff, right? Help us out."

I nod.

"I was telling your dad about an old buddy of ours,

Mike Arbol. He was really into pumping iron like you when he was younger and now he's got all sorts of heart problems. I think it's from all those years of lifting weights but your dad thinks—"

"Buuuuullshiiiiiiiit. Mike Arbol started smoking before we did!" Dad says. "And that guy drinks more than the three of us combined!"

"No, no," Keith says. "Let Dylan talk, he'll know about this stuff."

"Well..." I say. I scan between Dad's eyes, Keith's eyes and Dan's eyes, searching for my words.

"I'm with my Dad on this one, Keith. I don't think working out could've screwed up his heart. Unless this Mike Arbol guy was on the juice or something."

"Ah, well. you know. I thought from pumping iron all that time, you know, his heart pumping all that blood, you know..." Keith trails off and takes a swig of his beer.

"I think these puppies are done," I say as I transfer the sausages onto the top rack of the grill.

"I'm gonna take a leak before we eat," Keith says, getting up from his seat. He walks to-wards the door and stumbles over the doorjamb as he enters the house.

"Dad, do we have paper plates?" I ask.

"Yeah, under the sink in the kitchen. Grab the buns too, please," Dad says, gulping down another mouthful of beer.

I dial down the burners on the barbeque and close the

heavy stainless steel lid. I amble through the back door, pass through the living room and turn the corner towards the kitchen. Keith stands on his tippy toes reaching for the shelf above the fridge where Dad keeps his medication.

"What are you doing?" I ask.

Keith rips his arm down, knocking a pill bottle from its place. It bursts open as it hits the dark green vinyl flooring. Several little white Oxycontins roll around my feet.

"Uh, your dad..." he says. "He said his foot was bothering him. I was getting his pills."

Lighter
Hiba Traboulsi

Fire spreads over my uncle's massage chair as I tiptoe down the dim hallway to the kitchen, trying not to wake anyone. My toes burn and my legs wobble. I fall forward, scraping my knees on the tile.

I crawl to the sink. I fill a cup with water and scurry back to the storage room, keeping my eyes on the overflowing cup, cautious not to spill a drop. I breathe deeply with every step.

"It's okay," I tell myself. "I got this under control."

I turn into the storage room, ready to extinguish the flames with the water in the cup. I splash water at the fire. It hisses back and the red flames climb higher. I rush back to the kitchen and grab two cups this time, and race back. Water splashes over the rim of the cup and I slow down.

I throw more water on the fire and the flames erupt. They crackle and spill over and onto a black sofa, slowly stripping away its cover. The expanding embers eat away another blanket from another piece of furniture, revealing my grandma's old stowed-away rugs, antique armchairs and wooden side tables. The fire creeps along the rest of the mismatched sofas that square the storage room.

I never should have played with my uncle's lighter.

Plan A is failing, and I don't have a plan B. I hear the shuffling sound of someone walking outside the room. I leap across the room and swing the door behind me just in time to hide everything from my grandmother. The heat stings my back.

She smiles and walks to the kitchen. I wipe the sweat from my forehead and walk across the hallway and into the living room. My aunt watches my four-year-old cousin Khalid play with his Legos while my grandfather sleeps in his chair. I walk through the room and sit on the floor next to Khalid.

I cross my legs, digging my ankles into the woolly argyle carpet that blankets the marble floor. I watch as my grandmother shuffles into the living room, balancing a cup of hot tea in her hand. I gulp and tap my fingers on the soles of my feet, unsure of what to say.

I look around at family pictures that frame the walls of the lofty room. I glare at the red sofa ahead of me. The daffodil on the near side-table has shriveled and bent in half. The clock behind it strikes louder with every second.

My grandmother sits in front of me. She sets down her tea, places an arm around me and squeezes.

"Love you, my little angel," Grandmother says as she plants a kiss on my forehead. I smile and return her hug.

Grandmother turns to my aunt and they begin to discuss soap operas.

I peer at the storage room from where I sit and notice the smoke escaping the one-inch gap that I left open. I pray that no one else notices.

Khalid turns around and darts out of the room. His Lego fort stands high. He freezes in front of the burning door.

"So, what are we having for dinner tonight?" I squeal, trying to distract my family.

Grandmother's face lights up. She rambles on about her tasty shawarma sandwiches, crunchy spring rolls, and sweet lentil soup. I nod with enthusiasm.

"Oh—my—god," my aunt mouths the words.

She leaps off the couch, knocking over Khalid's Lego fort. The loud shatter startles grandpa and wakes him from his sleep.

I look up at Khalid's small body outlined before a red ring of fire. Bright flashes of orange fill the storage room.

My grandmother snatches a heavy blanket to smother the fire and sprints out of the room. I've never seen grandmother run.

I feel my head get lighter as my aunt drags a gallon-sized bucket of water into the room. My aunt and my grandmother both grasp onto the handle and throw the water at the flames. They take turns running in and out, grabbing more and more water.

My uncle's blue massage chair is now black and covered in ash. Broken glass litters the floor and jagged pieces hang from the frame of the two windows.

My aunt and my grandmother stare at me, at what I've done and at the lighter I left lying on the floor.

The Blue Cloth
Kristen Loritz

I stare at the pile of cornflakes floating in the ceramic bowl and smack my spoon against the rim. The edges of the golden flakes warp. They bob up and down in the milk.

The sun streams through the bay windows of the kitchen and I squint as I look out of them. Beyond my neighbor Julie's backyard fence, the green oak and maple trees of Kew Park tower over the narrow walkway that leads to Toronto's Kew Beach—a three-minute walk from my house. The wind whistles and hums. My screen door rattles.

Julie steps onto the worn wooden planks of her back deck. She turns southward, away from me, and faces the lake. She wraps her fingers around the metallic tumbler in her hands. Steam rises from the lid. She sips.

I follow her gaze across the park, through the trees, past the boardwalk, to the shores of Lake Ontario where the waves rise and fall. Julie crosses her arms and pulls her beige cardigan close to her body. She lifts her frail shoulders to her ears and shivers. A blue piece of fabric hugs Julie's head. It winds tightly around the crown and around the nape of her neck.

Julie knocked on our front door a few weeks ago. She and Mom talked for several hours. I watched from the top of our staircase as they chatted in the living room. Mom made tea.

I crept downstairs and asked Julie about the blue cloth.

"Had to go in for some treatment," she said. "Breast cancer, you know? But I will be okay." Julie's lips curled up. "Nothing cooler than a few battle scars."

※

Mom's soft hand cradles mine as we stroll through Kew Park, past the gazebo and baseball diamond to my backyard. We stop and sit on the roots of an old oak across from my fence. A black squirrel leaps from a branch onto a wire. His tail sways and his ears pull back as he hangs upside down. I laugh.

Mom smiles, strokes my fingers, and kisses my forehead.

"I just want you to know," Mom says. "I have cancer, but…"

Mom's slender nose lifts and points towards the lake.

We watch the waves in the distance crash onto the shore. Mom turns her head towards me. I see her face for the first time. Her once-round cheeks look gaunt and yellow and her once-soft hair looks brittle and tangled.

"It's not contagious," Mom says. "I will be okay."

"Promise?"

"I will do my best." Mom smiles.

"Like Julie?" I ask.

"Yes, sweetie. Just like Julie."

Mom rests her palms on my back and runs her fingers up and down my spine. I twist and giggle and squirm. Mom pulls me towards her and ruffles my hair.

"I am proud of you," she says. "You handled this so well."

Mom stands and takes my hand in hers. We walk in silence to our backyard. When we reach the gate, I run ahead, rip open the screen door and throw my school bag on the floor. My *Science 3* textbook slides out of my bag and smacks the hardwood floor and my notes fall out from between the pages. I crumple the papers and shove them into my bag.

Mom pulls the screen across the doorframe and steps inside. Dad crouches by the fridge. He pulls out a tray and strolls towards the kitchen table across from me.

"Hey! I made you—"

"I'm not hungry," I lie.

Dad shrugs and leaves the crackers and cheese on the

counter. I walk through our kitchen, into the hall and up the stairs. The hardwood creaks beneath my feet.

Why now? Why Mom?

❧

The next day, after school, I throw my bag on the steps in our front hallway. A wig hangs from the railing banister. The hair is black, cut shoulder-length with bangs, like Mom's. The wig hangs limp. Strands of hair drape across the banister and some pieces stick up. I feel nauseated.

Several weeks go by. The oaks and the maples of Kew Park shed their gold and red leaves, covering our backyard in a quilt of fiery colour.

A box of cornflakes rests on the kitchen table. I tilt the box. The tiny flakes fall into the bowl of milk. I hear a chattering sound resonate in my back door.

I look up and see Julie peel her screen door back and step onto her deck. She stares at the lake that shimmers under the September sun. A straw sunhat covers her head instead of the blue cloth. The rim droops and masks her profile. A large pink flower adorns the side. Julie crosses her arms and pulls her windbreaker close to her body. She lifts the same metallic tumbler to her lips and sips. An inch of brown hair peaks out from the nape of her neck. Julie tilts her head back and closes her eyes. She smiles.

❧

Mom's feet sink into the pillows of our white couch as she pulls down a life-size mummy from the front window. Frost crystals cling to the corners of the glass. Mom's breath fogs the pane.

"C'mon, take a break!" Mom calls. "Help us take down these decorations."

I watch from the adjacent couch as Mom tears a strand of blinking lights from the curtain rail. I shut my *Science 4* textbook, slide it off my lap and stand up.

I chuck a plastic spider at Nicole, my five-year-old sister, across the room. Nicole screams and tosses the spider. It lands on Mom's shoulder. Nicole waves her arms, runs towards Mom, wrestles her, and howls with laughter. Nicole claws and tugs at Mom's top. The neckline plunges to reveal a pink line. The line runs across Mom's chest where her right breast should be. A rubber lump fills the void. Mom yanks up her shirt.

"Mommy, why do you keep doing that?" Nicole asks.

"Because you keep pulling it down!" Mom says as she flattens the wrinkles on her shirt. Nicole scrunches up her nose. I scratch my forearm until the skin turns pink like the line on Mom's chest. I stand up, knocking my textbook to the floor. My notes slide out.

I don't know much about cancer, but I think about the conversation I had with Mom. I think about Julie and the blue cloth. I think about the wig, and I think about Mom's words.

My face flushes and I walk out of the room.

ABOUT THE AUTHORS

Samantha Ashenhurst
Samantha Ashenhurst is in third year, majoring in professional writing and communication (PWC) and women and gender studies. Born and raised in Mississauga, Samantha earned her diploma in print journalism from Sheridan College in 2006. She has been published in different newspapers and journals. Her work has also been featured in *Showing the Story*, a collection of creative non-fiction pieces published through Life Rattle.

Laura Gillis
Laura Gillis is a second-year student majoring in Communication, Culture, Information and Technology (CCIT) and PWC. She wants to pursue a career in public relations. Laura likes to dance, travel, read and attend concerts. She has discovered how much she enjoys writing creative non-fiction over the past year because it allows memories to be brought to life again. This is Laura's first time being published and she hopes for more opportunities in the future.

Jill Kennedy
Jill Kennedy is a fourth-year Visual Culture and Communication specialist and PWC major. She enjoys spending time with her ragdoll cat, Freddie McConnell. This is her first time being published.

Kristen Loritz
Kristen Loritz grew up in the bohemian neighbourhood of the Toronto beaches. As a competitive figure skater, Kristen has earned six national titles and three world medals with the NEXXICE Senior synchronized skating team. She is in third year, pursing a CCIT major and a PWC minor. Kristen loves cooking, sketching, travelling and producing multimedia works.

Kevin Ludena

Kevin Ludena is a third-year commerce student specializing in accounting and minoring in PWC. He is the current Editor-in-Chief of the Undergraduate Commerce Society's quarterly magazine, *The Executive*. His creative inspiration range from Stephen Chbosky to Neil Gaiman. He dedicates this story included here to Chuck Jennings for being the first person to tell Kevin he could write, back in grade 12.

Rob Redford

Rob Redford is a fourth-year student who is excited to graduate this spring as a psychology specialist. He loves playing chess, watching stand-up comedy specials, practising guitar, reading books, listening to podcasts and drinking wine with his friends. Rob began writing stories in 2013 and is happy to have earned his first publication in *Mindwaves*.

Jai Sangha

Jai Sangha is an international student finishing a double major in PWC and mathematics. He was an Associate News Editor at the campus newspaper, *The Medium*, for the 2012/13 year, during which he published more than 30 articles. His story "Powering Canada" was published last year in *Writing History: A Collection by New Writers*.

Lyndsay Sinko

Lyndsay Sinko is a second-year student working towards a double major in English and PWC. She wants to pursue a career as an editor and writer. At 19 years old, Lyndsay coauthored and published a medieval fiction novel, *The New King*, through Amazon's CreateSpace feature. It is the first of seven anticipated novels in the series.

Dylan Smart
Dylan Smart is a fourth-year student studying PWC and psychology. Dylan enjoys creative non-fiction as well as science writing and contributing to his blog, entitled "Fitness101." Dylan aspires to a career in freelance fitness writing after earning certification as a strength and conditioning coach. Dylan has been published in UTM's scientific journal, *Compass*.

Matt Spadafora
Matt Spadafora is a fifth-year student pursuing PWC and English. He has worked as a residence don for two years. In April 2014, his book *Anatomy Lesson* will be published with Life Rattle. In his spare time, he likes to watch far too much TV, enjoy pepperoni pizza and envision what he'll say when he proposes to Jennifer Lawrence. This is his first time being published.

Hiba Traboulsi
Hiba Traboulsi is a third-year student majoring in psychology and PWC. Hiba likes to read, write, travel and run. She aspires to a career practising child psychology and writing for psychology magazines. This is Hiba's first time being published.